Integrating Science and Mathematics in the Elementary Curriculum

by
David M. Davison,
Kenneth W. Miller
and
Dixie L. Metheny

ISBN 0-87367-644-0
Copyright © 1999 by the Phi Delta Kappa Educational Foundation
Bloomington, Indiana

This fastback is sponsored by the University of North Dakota Chapter of Phi Delta Kappa International, which made a generous contribution toward publication costs.

The chapter sponsors this fastback on the occasion of the 75th anniversary of its founding to remember Joseph V. Breitweiser and Martelle L. Cushman and to honor John L. Whitcomb.

Table of Contents

Integration in the Elementary Curriculum 7

The Meaning of Integration 11
   Thematic Integration 12
   Science, Mathematics, and Children's
      Literature 14
   Integrating Science and Mathematics 16

**National Projects that Demonstrate
   Integration** 23
   AIMS (Activities Integrating Mathematics
      and Science) 23
   GEMS (Great Explorations in Math and
      Science) 24
   MAST (Math and Science Together) 25
   SIMMS (Systemic Initiative for Montana
      Mathematics and Science) 26
   TIMS (Teaching Integrated Mathematics
      and Science) 26
   TOPS 27
   Summary 28

**Paradigms in Science and Mathematics
   Integration** 29

Resources 33

Integration in the Elementary Curriculum

Today's schools are taking a more holistic view of teaching and learning than was the case in past decades. Therefore traditional approaches to structuring the curriculum are being reviewed, and disciplines often are being integrated to effect greater learning. Many discipline-focused organizations have published documents that reflect this altered view. For example, the trend toward holistic teaching is evident in *Curriculum and Evaluation Standards for School Mathematics* (National Council of Teachers of Mathematics 1989), *Benchmarks in Science* (American Association for the Advancement of Science 1993), and *National Science Education Standards* (National Research Council 1996).

These examples relate to science and mathematics — the focus of this fastback — but similar publications can be found in many disciplines. The view in these and similar documents is that the science and mathematics curricula should become more learner-oriented and relevant to students and that integration of the disciplines would facilitate such a reorientation. This is the view we adopt in suggesting that integration will contribute to a holistic approach to teaching and learning in elementary science and mathematics.

A perusal of the past decade's issues of the *Phi Delta Kappan* or other professional education journals should convince any reader that integrated, holistic learning has become the objective for curriculum reform and renewal. Evident in this direction for change are views that instruction should be more learner-centered than teacher-centered and that instruction is most effective when students are active rather than passive. Educators recognize that students need to *construct* knowledge, and thereby "own" it, rather than receive knowledge. Thus the teacher must change from being a disseminator of information to being a facilitator of student learning. Readers will recognize this altered view as an expression of constructivist theory. (For more information, see fastbacks 390 *Constructivist Teaching* and 435 *Constructivism and Science Teaching*.)

Integration may be interpreted in several ways. One interpretation is to integrate several disciplines around a unifying theme. Another is to integrate two or three disciplines, sometimes within the context of one of the included disciplines. And yet another interpretation is to blend subject matter generally. In this fastback we will examine all of these approaches in the adaptation of science and mathematics curricula.

A concern that we would express up front is that, while teachers and curricularists acknowledge the importance and validity of integrating science and mathematics, in fact little has happened to foster such integration in many classrooms. We have observed that science and mathematics — and most other disciplines — still are taught as separate curricula with little regard even for natural connections that might be made easily. Although integration is the stated position of the School Science and Mathematics Association, only a small number of the articles they publish actually deal with integration. Therefore it seems certain that teachers and curriculum developers could benefit from clarification and articulation of what integration means and why it should be made to happen.

In this fastback we examine some of the ways that integration of science and mathematics might be viewed. One such way is to consider how these disciplines have been interconnected throughout history, dating back to the earliest civilizations. In our most recent history, for example, the advances in space exploration are attributable largely to scientists' abilities to merge the disciplines of science and mathematics.

A second way to consider the integration of science and mathematics is to view such integration in these disciplines as an exemplar of similar integration that might take place in other disciplines. In this focus on the "hows" of integration, we show that integrative techniques can be applied to other subjects as successfully as to science and mathematics.

Finally, we review a number of existing programs that exemplify integration in science and mathematics. We connect this review to a look forward at ways of enhancing teaching and learning through greater understanding and application of integration. Our hope is that readers will take from this fastback a number of basic ideas about the integration of science and mathematics and will feel moved to pursue these approaches in their own school or classroom.

The Meaning of Integration

The term *integration* has been used in a variety of ways. For example, some educators interpret integration as a total blending of curricula from different disciplines. Jacobs (1989) reviews some of these variations of the "interdisciplinary curriculum." In one sense, an interdisciplinary curriculum may be fully holistic. In this sense science and mathematics — and other subjects — are subordinated to child-centered, rather than subject-centered, learning.

Another interdisciplinary curriculum approach is to blend science or mathematics, or both, with other subjects in the core curriculum, such as English and social studies. Although less "holistic" than the previous approach, this strategy places one or more subjects into the context of one or more other subjects. For example, science might be approached under the umbrella of social studies, taking up scientific principles in the context of their appearance in history. The reverse also might be true. English, for example, might be taken up in the context of science. A study of acids and bases might be the basis for doing research, reading stories with scientific content, and writing about classroom experiments.

Perhaps most common is the integration of science and mathematics by themselves, blending the two disciplines into a holistic science/math curriculum. This strategy often is seen as both logical and logistically feasible.

What follows in this section are several short discussions of these variations on the theme of integration. A number of factors will determine which, if any, "fit" a given school or classroom.

Thematic Integration

The use of a common theme for study is becoming increasingly popular in elementary schools that want to integrate two or more disciplines. Using thematic integration means taking up science and mathematics (and other subjects) incidentally within the holistic treatment of the theme.

Themes — such as air quality, space exploration, dinosaurs, etc. — are excellent motivators of student learning. Themes may be drawn from the day's news or traditional subject matter in any discipline. McDonald and Czerniak (1994) point out that conversations among students can provide teachers with cues about themes that may engage student interest and arouse curiosity.

An example theme might be air quality. The science applications are obvious: chemistry, environmental studies, biology. Considering the human ramifications, legal concerns, and sociological factors related to air quality would tie the theme to social studies. For English, or language arts, students might read newspaper and magazine articles about air quality and write reports about their findings. For mathematics, students might calculate levels of sulfur dioxide. For art, students might create air quality awareness posters or seek out scenic paintings and discuss the air quality evident in the scenes. For music, students might listen to protest songs and write their own lyrics to protest air pollution.

While thematic integration is a valuable way to have a variety of disciplines addressed through a single theme, teachers need to be sure that each subject is dealt with in a meaningful way. With some themes this goal is easier to achieve than with others. There is a danger that one or more disciplines may be addressed only superficially. Another superficiality issue concerns whether important knowledge and understandings in each discipline can be covered using thematic integration. For example, calculating levels of sulfur dioxide, while an interesting application of mathematical skill, may have little to do with the actual math learning objectives of the particular grade level. Similarly, if this thematic unit is, say, for third-graders, then even though science and mathematics might well be used extensively in the study of air quality, the useful level of science and mathematics is too advanced for third grade.

These concerns should not discourage teachers from using thematic integration, but it probably should not be the sole vehicle for making decisions about curriculum content. Thematic integration is perhaps most readily used *to apply* knowledge and understandings acquired in discipline-focused study. For example, a thematic unit based on the Lewis and Clark expedition, while primarily a social studies topic, can be used extensively to enhance students' application of science knowledge (studying Lewis' records of wildlife and flora) and math skills (calculating quantities and costs of expedition provisions). These are excellent applications, but thematic integration is seldom as useful to introduce new information in science and mathematics.

Science, Mathematics, and Children's Literature

Broad thematic integration may be best used for application of science and mathematics knowledge, but other, more selective forms of integration may be better suited both to learning basic skills and to performing higher-level thinking activities. For example, science and mathematics might be placed in the fore of the curriculum, with children's literature made to serve as the vehicle for application and extension.

Children will enjoy reading David Schwartz's *How Much Is a Million?* (William Morrow, 1985) as an introduction to talking about large numbers. A class might calculate, for instance, how far a string of one million pennies would stretch. One fifth-grade class we know used HyperStudio to create a computer presentation to demonstrate their understandings of large numbers. (For other computer applications, see fastback 445 *Project-Based Multimedia Instruction*.)

Many children's books can be adapted for teaching mathematics concepts. Another example is Ann Tompert's *Grandfather Tang's Story* (Crown, 1990). This story centers on the making of tangrams, which introduce children to geometric shapes. A follow-up activity after reading Tompert's book might be to have students create their own tangrams and write their own stories.

Children's literature also can be useful to teach and reinforce science instruction. This can be especially true when it comes to correcting students' prior misconceptions. Miller, Steiner, and Larson (1996) identify four steps in helping students become aware of and correct misconceptions about science knowledge. First, teachers need to identify the misconception. Second, they must confront the misconception through inquiry ("What do you mean by... ?"). Third, teachers must provide students with experiences that challenge the misconception and present the correct concept. And, fourth, teachers need to reinforce the new, correct concept by giving students ample evidence of its validity.

Children's literature can set up the "test" for misconceptions. For example, Verna Aardema's *Bringing the Rain to Kapiti Plain* (Dial, 1981) tells a story about rain resulting from holes being shot into clouds. This offers a "setup" to talk about how rain actually does happen. The students can even conduct simple experiments to demonstrate how rain is formed. Then, to provide more evidence of the correct concept, students can read Eleanore Schmid's *The Water's Journey* (North-South, 1989) or David Bennett's *Rain* (Bantam, 1988), which portray the true cycle of rain formation.

A version of this type of integration, wherein science or mathematics (or both) takes the foreground, is evident in most science and mathematics textbooks nowadays. The emerging emphasis on integration and holistic curriculum has put social studies concepts, literature concepts, and so forth, into the textbook lessons. Where the integration is not as apparent in the student texts, it is integral to the teacher's editions, which often contain suggestions for relating textbook lessons to children's literature, health and nutrition, history, and the like.

Integrating Science and Mathematics

Most of the attention to integration in science and mathematics is given to merging, in one form or another, these two disciplines by themselves, rather than with other disciplines. Indeed, this more limited type of integration is probably easiest to accomplish and most likely to include the full range of knowledge that should be taught and learned in each subject.

Lonning and DeFranco (1994, 1997) view the integration of science and mathematics as a continuum. At one end stands "independent science," meaning no integration of mathematics. The next step along the continuum is "science focus," mostly science with some integration of mathematics. The midpoint is "balanced science and mathematics"; the continuum then moves to "mathematics focus," with some science; and finally, at the other end, "independent mathematics." As they worked with this notion of a continuum, Lonning and

DeFranco concluded that "certain science and mathematics concepts are best taught independently, while others lend themselves to natural integration, that is, relevant science activities utilizing meaningful mathematics skills" (1994, p. 20).

Berlin and White have long been acknowledged as leaders in the movement to integrate science and mathematics. Berlin's (1991) annotated bibliography of science and mathematics integration resources is worth recommending to readers interested in pursuing this topic in depth. The Berlin-White Integrated Science and Mathematics (BWISM) Model identifies six aspects of integration: 1) ways of learning, 2) ways of knowing, 3) process and thinking skills, 4) content knowledge, 5) attitudes and perceptions, and 6) teaching strategies (Berlin and White 1994, 1995). Berlin and White assert that "if educators are to explore and harness the potential of the integration of science and mathematics education, a common language must first be established" (1994, p. 2). They stress the need for a definition on which educators can agree.

Davison, Miller, and Metheny (1995) propose a categorical approach to classifying different ways of integrating science and mathematics. The categories are discipline-specific integration, content-specific integration, thematic integration (discussed in the previous section), and process integration. This categorization is compatible with Lonning and DeFranco's continuum but allows the user to think in somewhat different terms about ways to implement integration.

Discipline-specific integration denotes integration that occurs entirely within a single discipline. Both science and mathematics comprise numerous disciplines (or subdisciplines). In science, for example, discipline-specific integration might mean integrating biology, chemistry, and physics. In mathematics, it might mean integrating algebra and geometry.

Because this integration is "intra-" science or "intra-" mathematics, it exemplifies the ends of the continuum suggested by Lonning and DeFranco. And yet, it is a real form of integration, because traditionally the subdisciplines of science and mathematics have been taught separately. Thus such integration is a strategy for teaching holistic science and holistic mathematics.

An application of holistic science can be seen in the example of a unit on pollution. Students might study types of pollutants and how they can be eliminated or cleaned up. The unit might include gaseous, liquid, and solid pollutants. Students might, for instance, set out cups of water, add various pollutants, and then experiment with clean-up methods. By various means the students can touch on several science disciplines: biology, ecology, and chemistry, for starters.

In mathematics, a similar integration might involve the study of number patterns. Traditionally this topic is presented in the abstract, but students learn about number patterns more readily when they can apply them and play with them. To get to the notion of $1+2+3+4+5+6+\ldots+n = n(n+1)/2$, students might consider adding two sequences: $1+2+3+4+5+6+7+8$ and $8+7+6+5+4+3+2+1$. This yields $9+9+9+9+9+9+9+9$; thus the double sum is 8 x 9, and the sum of the sequence is (8 x 9)/2. Students can explore to derive the generalization themselves, and they can obtain the geometric equivalent using unifix cubes, Cuisenaire rods, or other manipulatives.

Young children similarly can explore whole numbers, fractions, and decimals using objects as well as written numbers. For example, students might work in groups to examine relationships among body parts. Is the circumference of a person's neck twice the circumference of his or her wrist? Conjecture-and-test applications can help students learn about making and testing hypotheses.

Content-specific integration is the term we use to denote the linking of a science objective with a mathematics objective in a single lesson. In this way integration conforms to the scope and sequence of both disciplines. Such integration may take place even when science and mathematics are taught in different classrooms by different teachers.

Content-specific integration can be seen by laying side-by-side the curricula for science and mathematics classes and then structuring lessons so that objectives coincide in actuality as well as in theory. On the Lonning-DeFranco continuum, this strategy may be considered "science focus" or "mathematics focus," depending on the class in question. Or, holistically, it may be considered "balanced."

The unit approach in elementary schools again is useful for content-specific integration. For example, in a unit on dinosaurs the students might study the various animals, their environments, and so on, in science class. Then, in math class, the students might recreate two or three dinosaurs using masking tape to form their outlines on a gymnasium floor and then using a variety of measurement skills to calculate the sizes and size relationships of the dinosaurs.

Older elementary students might investigate the solar system and its characteristics in science and then create mathematically accurate models or diagrams in mathematics, using concepts of scale and proportion.

A water rocket unit can be used in similar fashion, except in this case the hands-on activity occurs in science. Students assemble water rockets using liter-size plastic bottles, water, and an air pump. They construct sighting devices using meter sticks, protractors, and weighted strings and observe the upward climb of their rockets. Then, in mathematics, they use graph paper to chart rocket courses and to compare successful and unsuccessful "firings."

Content-specific integration offers many opportunities, such as those described, to pair science and mathematics learning along the lines of similar or related objectives. But, as is the case with any form of integration, a word of caution is necessary. Such integration should not be forced. Not every objective in science will match one in mathematics, and vice versa. Where integration can be accomplished, it should be; but not every objective will lend itself to integrated learning.

Process integration refers not to science or mathematics content, but to processes associated with both of these disciplines. The standards in both mathematics and science suggest that processes are as important as content, and the integration of processes often is central to understanding science and mathematics content. Drawing on the standards from the National Council of Teachers of Mathematics (1989) and the National Research Council (1996), the following chart illustrates the process elements that may be integrated:

Table 1. Process Integration.

Scientific Process	K-4 Mathematics Standards

• Experimenting
  Observing
  Predicting
  Inferring
  Testing hypotheses
  Controlling variables
	• Problem Solving
	  Reasoning
	  Estimation

• Communication	• Communication
• Using Space Relationships	• Geometry and Spatial Sense Patterns and relationships
• Relevancy	• Connections

• Using Numbers	• Number Sense and Numeracy
	  Whole number operations
	  Whole number computation
	  Fractions and decimals

• Measuring	• Measurement
• Interpreting Data	• Statistics and Probability
• Classifying	• Classifying
• Defining Operationally	• Defining Operationally
• Using Time Relationships	• Using Time Relationships

Process integration is exemplified in helping students to demonstrate "scientific thinking." One way to approach this activity is to ask students to investigate a question or topic that is relevant to them. A good source for questions or topics is *Consumer Reports* magazine. The editors of *Consumer Reports*, for example, might pose the question: Which is the best athletic shoe? This is certainly a relevant question for middle school students, who might then be led to make comparisons among various types of athletic shoes: court shoes, running shoes, tennis shoes, and so on. They might test the "drag-ability" of the shoes by dragging them across various surfaces using a spring balance. Which shoes fare best on blacktop, wood floors, carpet, and tile?

The students also might chart the various types of shoes according to appearance (style), comfort, brand-name appeal, and price. We have found that it is important for students to arrive at their own criteria and product tests, because making such decisions allows them to take ownership of the processes. When the students have finished their investigations, they summarize their findings and prepare a presentation, often comparing their tests to the results obtained by the *Consumer Reports* testers.

The importance of giving students ownership in process integration cannot be overemphasized. In fact, we believe that students operating in this constructivist model of learning actually move systematically on their own through a cycle of four stages: 1) defining a topic or question of interest, 2) exploring the topic, 3) attaining new concepts, and 4) applying new understanding to the topic or question (Renner and Marek 1988).

National Projects that Demonstrate Integration

In this section we briefly discuss six projects that illustrate ways of integrating science and mathematics. The projects may be best known by their acronyms: AIMS, GEMS, MAST, SIMMS, TIMS, and TOPS.

AIMS (Activities Integrating Mathematics and Science)

Various activities are provided for kindergarten through grade nine in the AIMS materials (from AIMS, P.O. Box 8120, Fresno, CA 93747. Phone: 202/291-1766). These activities include detailed lesson plans for teachers and motivating worksheets for students. A good example is the AIMS book, *Critters*, designed for grades K-6. It begins with a list of mathematics skills and science processes that will be developed through the lessons in the book. The introductory lesson, called "Home on the Range," lets the students select homes for several types of animals, including a butterfly, an ant, a snake, and a turtle. Home choices include a liter bottle with holes in the top, a jar, a milk carton, and a plastic shoe box.

Critters illustrates process integration. For example, in the lesson called "Animal Antics," students begin classifying animals into phyla and classes. They practice observation in the science framework. Then, in the math framework they make calculations and create graphs based on a system of numerical scores for the various animals.

While AIMS lessons offer some advantages, they sometimes miss crucial elements of process integration. Curricular content for both science and mathematics tends to be minimal, and the activities are highly structured. Teachers are expected to use a "cookbook" approach, and few decisions are left to students. In true process integration we would hope to see greater student involvement and ownership of ideas and activities. A constructivist approach would emphasize teachers and students working more collaboratively, so that students could define their own questions and devise their own strategies for answering them.

GEMS (Great Explorations in Math and Science)

The GEMS activities are created by the Lawrence Hall of Science at the University of California at Berkeley and are designed for grades four through eight. They follow a discipline-specific model of integration.

The GEMS book, *Oobleck*, illustrates discipline-specific integration of chemistry and physics, for example.

Students investigate the properties of Oobleck, a substance made of cornstarch, water, and green food coloring. Lessons include describing the properties of Oobleck, arriving at the "laws of Oobleck," and designing a spacecraft that could land on a sea of Oobleck. Students also talk about the processes they use throughout the lessons.

MAST (Math and Science Together)

As part of the Statewide Systemic Initiative Program funded by the National Science Foundation, the Arkansas MAST Project developed lessons for grades two through six. These lessons use many commercially available materials in innovative ways and illustrate thematic integration.

For example, the unit on "Family" includes 45 lessons and begins by enumerating the special features of each lesson, such as whether the lesson includes manipulatives, its appropriateness for special populations, whether students must use a computer or calculator, and so forth. Several lessons involve cooperative groups, include parents, and incorporate a multicultural perspective. The lessons also are tied to the National Council of Teachers of Mathematics K-4 curriculum and evaluation standards and to the Arkansas math and science standards.

The "big idea" for the first lesson is "Animal Families," which follows a theme of dinosaurs. The guiding question is, What does extinction mean? This question will change with each lesson. Students will engage in activities related to language arts, reading, math, science, and physical education. The lesson includes information on the causes of extinction, habitat loss and degradation, and other factors. Students arrive at their own conclusions about how dinosaurs became extinct.

This variation of thematic integration maintains the curriculum for each subject area, but it runs the risk of trivializing attention to the thematic topic.

SIMMS (Systemic Initiative for Montana Mathematics and Science)

The SIMMS curriculum consists of integrated mathematics and science materials for grades nine through 12, but many of the activities can be easily adapted for middle-grades students. The SIMMS materials contain many components that exemplify discipline-specific integration.

For example, the "Giants" module integrates algebra and geometry, beginning with a study of proportion. Students start the unit by measuring the foot lengths and heights of themselves and their classmates. Then they develop ratios and arrive at a general formula, which they use to predict the foot length or height of other students, teachers, and parents. Later activities include using proportions to solve for missing information. The "science" in this project is to provide a real-life context for the application of mathematical concepts.

TIMS (Teaching Integrated Mathematics and Science)

The TIMS project was funded by the National Science Foundation and resulted in the development of Math

Trailblazers, a curriculum for grades one through six. The materials are now published commercially by Kendall/Hunt.

In the TIMS materials the primary goal is to produce students who are excited about mathematics, comfortable with mathematics, and flexible in their math thinking. Ideally, the students will come to see connections between the mathematics they learn in school and the thinking they do in everyday life. The series of lessons develops students' understanding of mathematical concepts with applications to science and language arts.

TOPS

The TOPS booklets are produced by TOPS Learning Systems in Canby, Oregon. Each booklet covers a different topic, such as metric measurement, pendulums, or floating and sinking. The booklets feature extensive teacher notes and reproducible student activity sheets.

One of the booklets in the TOPS series is titled, "Metric Measuring." It begins with a list of materials for a resource center and discusses both an individualized approach to the topic and a traditional class lesson. The activities lead the students through a study of length, area, and volume in the metric system. The final activities involve mass, liquid measure, and density.

TOPS booklets are easy for teachers to use. The needed materials tend to be readily available and inexpensive. And the activities will engage the interest of students through process integration. Attention to the science processes and mathematics standards is evident, and there is an orientation to "best practice" in both disciplines. The TOPS materials are designed for use primarily in elementary science, and so the mathematics components mainly serve to enhance the science.

Summary

These projects have the potential to integrate mathematics and science in varying degrees. The AIMS materials illustrate process integration, GEMS materials incorporate discipline-specific integration, and the MAST materials integrate various disciplines based on a theme. But in many of the TIMS materials it is difficult see the integration of language arts and science for the overwhelming emphasis on math, and the TOPS materials usually involve only one subject area. SIMMS materials are appropriate for integrating the mathematics disciplines but must be adapted for younger students. These factors should be kept in mind when decisions about integration models are made.

Paradigms in Science and Mathematics Integration

Understanding the paradigms of science and mathematics integration is important in making decisions about integrating subject matter and processes. Two paradigms, the technical and the practical, adapted from the work of Schwab (1969), and Grundy (1987), reflect methods of thinking about integration that may be helpful to this understanding.

The technical paradigm encourages thinking based on achieving a product, usually with the learner taking a passive role. The teacher is viewed as a dispenser of information, and classroom instruction typically is delivered by lecture and discussion. Focus in the technical paradigm is on content mastery; therefore integration is targeted to this goal, and achievement is measured using criterion- and norm-referenced tests.

By contrast the practical paradigm frames teaching and learning in terms of processes that encourage inquiry and discovery. Students are encouraged to become involved in making decisions about instruction. The teacher is viewed as a facilitator. Focus in the practical paradigm is on processes through which students achieve new understandings; consequently, assessment turns on the use of rubrics specific to various projects, performance-based testing, and portfolios.

Current research suggests that educators would better serve their students by adopting the practical paradigm, focusing on the learner and how his or her learning can be facilitated, rather than focusing on the teacher and how to "teach better." This notion of the practical paradigm is consistent with constructivist theory.

Constructivist models of teaching and learning advocate building on initial understandings and a development of meaning that is individually generated. The role of the teacher is one of a facilitator or guide. Yager (1991) reminds us that such instruction may be very different from many teachers' own school experiences. The strategies of constructivist teaching, to the untrained eye, sometimes appear to be haphazard, especially when compared to the more controlled, teacher-centered (technical paradigm), traditional classrooms (Grundy 1987). Nevertheless, there has been — and continues to be — a shift away from the technical paradigm and toward the practical paradigm. This shift is global and concomitant with the shift from an industrial economy to an information and service economy that depends on people skills, teamwork, and information gathering and processing (Miller et al. 1996).

Can teachers go too far with the practical paradigm? Probably. A complete de-emphasis of teacher-focused instruction can deprive students of essential guidance. Direct instruction can be positive and beneficial, even within an overall orientation toward the practical paradigm. But many educators argue that the technical paradigm, with its focus on content objectives and teacher-oriented instruction, when unmodified by the practical paradigm, fails to prepare students to be able to think critically, to work cooperatively, and to solve problems.

The standards written for science and mathematics education are consistent with the practical paradigm, and yet many textbooks continue to assign greater value to "right" answers (products) and knowledge acquisition than to knowledge construction (process) (Costa and Liebmann 1995). In fact, many textbooks claim to contain methods, emphases, and content that focus on meeting the standards; but, in fact, they differ little from the technical paradigm texts of the past.

Thus it falls mainly to educators to provide relevant connections among disciplines and to design meaningful integration that enhances student ownership of learning. Counting paramecia under a microscope, in spite of what the teacher's edition may claim, is not a meaningful integration of science and math. Nor is reading about whales in the *Weekly Reader* a meaningful integration of science and reading.

Constructing knowledge means identifying what knowledge is important and designing ways for students to participate in the identification, acquisition, and construction processes. We argue that meaningful integration is one way of amplifying and intensifying this construction process.

In this fastback we have discussed various types of integration of mathematics and science, examined the corresponding teaching and learning methods required for integration, and discussed the essential paradigms. We have considered the integration of science and mathematics from the standpoint of integrating these disciplines into a holistic curriculum, integrating other areas of the curriculum into the science and mathematics curricula, and integrating science and mathematics with each other. We also have considered projects that exemplify these different approaches to integration. All of this, we hope, offers starting points for thinking about how integration of science and mathematics can be accomplished in the elementary curriculum.

Resources

American Association for the Advancement of Science. *Benchmarks in Science*. New York: Oxford University Press, 1993.

Berlin, Donna F. "A Bibliography of Integrated Science and Mathematics Teaching and Learning Literature." *School Science and Mathematics Association Topics for Teachers Series* Number 6. Columbus, Ohio: ERIC Clearinghouse for Science, Mathematics and Environmental Education, 1991.

Berlin, Donna F., and White, Arthur L. "The Berlin-White Integrated Science and Mathematics Model." *School Science and Mathematics* 94 (January 1994): 2-4.

Berlin, Donna F., and White, Arthur L. "Connecting School Science and Mathematics." In *Connecting Mathematics Across the Curriculum*, edited by Peggy A. House and Arthur F. Coxford. Reston, Va.: National Council of Teachers of Mathematics, 1995.

Costa, Arthur, and Liebmann, Rosemarie. "Process Is as Important as Content." *Educational Leadership* 52 (March 1995): 23-24.

Davison, David M.; Miller, Kenneth W.; and Metheny, Dixie L. "What Does the Integration of Mathematics and Science Really Mean?" *School Science and Mathematics* 95 (May 1995): 226-30.

Grundy, Shirley. *Curriculum: Product or Praxis?* New York: Falmer Press, 1987.

Jacobs, Heidi Hayes, ed. *Interdisciplinary Curriculum*. Alexandria, Va.: Association for Supervision and Curriculum Development, 1989.

Lonning, Robert A., and DeFranco, Thomas C. "Development and Implementation of an Integrated Mathematics/Science Preservice Elementary Methods Course." *School Science and Mathematics* 94 (January 1994): 18-25.

Lonning, Robert A., and DeFranco, Thomas C. "Integration of Science and Mathematics: A Theoretical Model." *School Science and Mathematics* 97 (April 1997): 212-15.

McDonald, Jacqueline, and Czerniak, Charlene. "Developing Interdisciplinary Units: Strategies and Examples." *School Science and Mathematics* 94 (January 1994): 5-10.

Miller, Kenneth W. "Paradigmatic School Philosophies as Barriers to School Reform." *Science Educator* 5 (Spring 1996): 1-6.

Miller, Kenneth W., and Davison, David. "Is Thematic Integration the Best Way to Reform Science and Mathematics Education?" *Science Educator* 7 (Spring 1998): 7-12.

Miller, Kenneth; Davison, David; and Metheny, Dixie. "Integrating Mathematics and Science at the Middle School Level." *Montana Mathematics Teacher* 6 (Fall 1993): 3-7.

Miller, Kenneth; Metheny, Dixie; and Davison, David. "Issues in Integrating Mathematics and Science." *Science Educator* 6 (Spring 1997): 16-21.

Miller, Kenneth; Steiner, Stanley; and Larson, Carol. "Strategies for Science Learning." *Science and Children* 33 (March 1996): 24-28.

National Council of Teachers of Mathematics. *Curriculum and Evaluation Standards for School Mathematics*. Reston, Va., 1989.

National Research Council. *National Science Education Standards*. Washington, D.C., 1996.

Renner, John W., and Marek, Edmund A. *The Learning Cycle*. Portsmouth, N.H.: Heinemann, 1988.

Schwab, Joseph J. "The Practical: A Language for Curriculum." *School Review* 78 (November 1969): 1-23.

Yager, Robert E. "The Constructivist Learning Model." *Science Teacher* 58 (September 1991): 52-57.

Project Materials

Allen, Maureen; Deal, Debby; Kahn, Gale; Scheidt, Suzanne; and Sipkovich, Vincent. *Critters*. Fresno, Calif.: AIMS Education Foundation, 1992.

Arkansas Project MAST. University of Arkansas. Little Rock, 1997.

Great Explorations in Math and Science. *Oobleck: What Do Scientists Do?* Berkeley, Calif.: Lawrence Hall of Science, 1985.

Marson, Ron. *Metric Measuring*. Canby, Ore.: TOPS Learning Systems, 1984.

Montana Council of Teacher of Mathematics. *Systemic Initiative for Montana Mathematics and Science*. Bozeman, 1993.

TIMS Project. *Math Trailblazers*. Dubuque: Kendall/Hunt, 1997.

Trade Books

Aardema, Verna. *Bringing the Rain to Kapiti Plain*. New York: Dial, 1981.

Bennett, David. *Rain*. Toronto: Bantam, 1988.

Schwartz, David. *How Much Is a Million?* New York: William Morrow & Company, 1985.

Schmid, Eleanore. *The Water's Journey*. New York: North-South, 1989.

Tompert, Ann. *Grandfather Tang's Story*. New York: Crown, 1990.